W9-CEW-301

A GOOD DAY FOR
LISTENING

WRITTEN AND ILLUSTRATED
BY
MARY ELLEN KING

MOREHOUSE PUBLISHING
Harrisburg, PA

Morehouse Publishing
Editorial Office:
871 Ethan Allen Hwy.
Ridgefield, CT 06877

Corporate Office:
P.O. Box 1321
Harrisburg, PA 17105

ISBN: 0-8192-1638-0

Library of Congress Cataloging-in-Publication Data

King, Mary Ellen
    A good day for listening / written and illustrated by Mary Ellen King.
      p.   cm.
    Summary: Theodore the bear is a good listener, but his brother Benjamin is too busy thinking about his worries and misses out on a lot.
    ISBN 0-8192-1638-0
    [1. Listening—Fiction. 2. Brothers—Fiction. 3. Bears—Fiction] I. Title
PZ7.K5869Go   1995   [E]—dc20 94-49616
                                      CIP
                                      AC

Printed in Malaysia

For... My Dad and Mom
who taught me the value of listening
and
for my husband, Bill
and my children, Alyssa and Anna
who blend listening with love
every day.

It had just stopped raining and outside
was a morning drenched with puddles.
Bright drops of rain dripped from leafy treetops.

Drip. Drip.

It was a good day for listening.

"Wear your boots," Mama said as Theodore and Benjamin got ready for school. Theodore listened to his mother and snuggled his feet into his warm boots. Buckling them tightly, he Knew the boots would Keep him dry on his walk to school.

But Benjamin did not listen to his mother.
He didn't hear her mention his boots. Out the
door he marched with his bare bear feet,
sloshing through puddle after puddle. Soon
he was very wet and discouraged. "Oh,
puddles!" complained Benjamin. "Wet feet are
just unbearable!"

It wasn't long before Theodore heard
a bird singing near the playground.

Tweet. Tweet.

He stopped to listen to its beautiful song
and to watch it swoop and soar through
the sky. It made him smile and feel happy.
"I wonder what it would be like to fly,"
he thought.

Benjamin did not listen to the bird. He was in too much of a hurry to get to school so he could dry his soaked and chilly feet. He didn't notice the bird at all. "Oh, no," Benjamin said, feeling grumpy. "I hope I don't catch a cold!"

That afternoon, the sun began to peek through the clouds. While they sat at their desks, their teacher told them about a far away land. Theodore listened with wonder and thought about what adventures he might have in such a new place. But Benjamin did not listen. He felt sleepy. He closed his eyes and didn't learn a thing.

After school, on the way home, Theodore heard a small sound.

Meow. Meow.

He listened carefully and discovered a frightened kitten that was caught in a bush. He freed the kitten and stroked her soft fur. They became friends.

But Benjamin just sat on his front steps.
He didn't hear the kitten. He didn't hear
anything. He was much too busy wishing he
had more friends. "It sure would be nice
to have someone to play with," he thought.

That night, as the sun went down in the sky, Papa read a funny story to Theodore and Benjamin. Theodore listened and giggled with delight. But Benjamin only pretended to listen. He was really thinking that the whole day hadn't been quite right. He felt sad and out-of-sorts. "Maybe tomorrow will be better," he thought.

Bedtime arrived. Theodore heard crickets chirping outside the window. It was a clear, bright night and the moon hung big in the sky.

Benjamin climbed onto his bed and grabbed his favorite blanket. He sighed a big sigh and pushed away all the hurry and worry from his day. Then he sat... quietly... for several moments. Everything was still except for the quiet song of the crickets. It was peaceful.

"Goodnight, Benjamin," Theodore whispered. "Are you listening? I love you!"

Benjamin snuggled down beneath his blanket. A big, slow smile came across his face. For the first time that day, Benjamin had listened and it was wonderful. "I love you too," he whispered back.

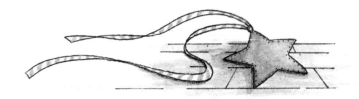

...And they both listened to the crickets
as they drifted off to sleep.

It was a good night for listening.